THE Life-Size GUIDE TO NATIVE TREES

and other common plants of New Zealand's native forest

Andrew Crowe

PENGUIN BOOKS

What have you found?

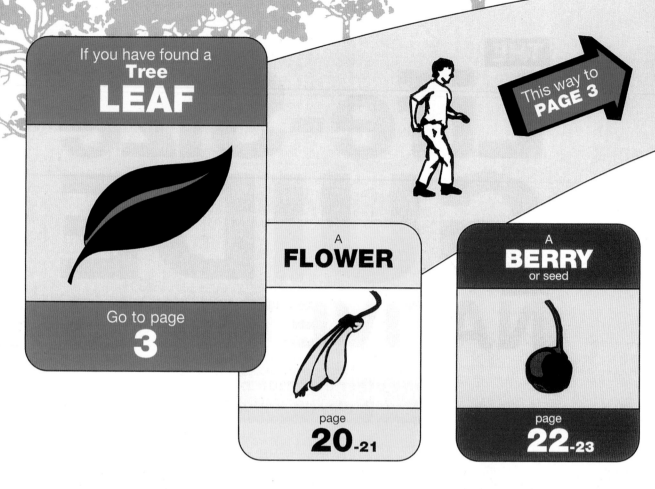

If you have found a
Tree
LEAF

Go to page
3

This way to
PAGE 3

A
FLOWER

page
20-21

A
BERRY
or seed

page
22-23

Tree
BARK

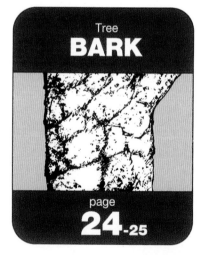

page
24-25

A plant
UP
in the trees

page
26-27

A plant
DOWN
on the forest floor

page
28-31

GLOSSARY
& BOOKS

page
31

INDEX

A
B
C

HELP

page
32

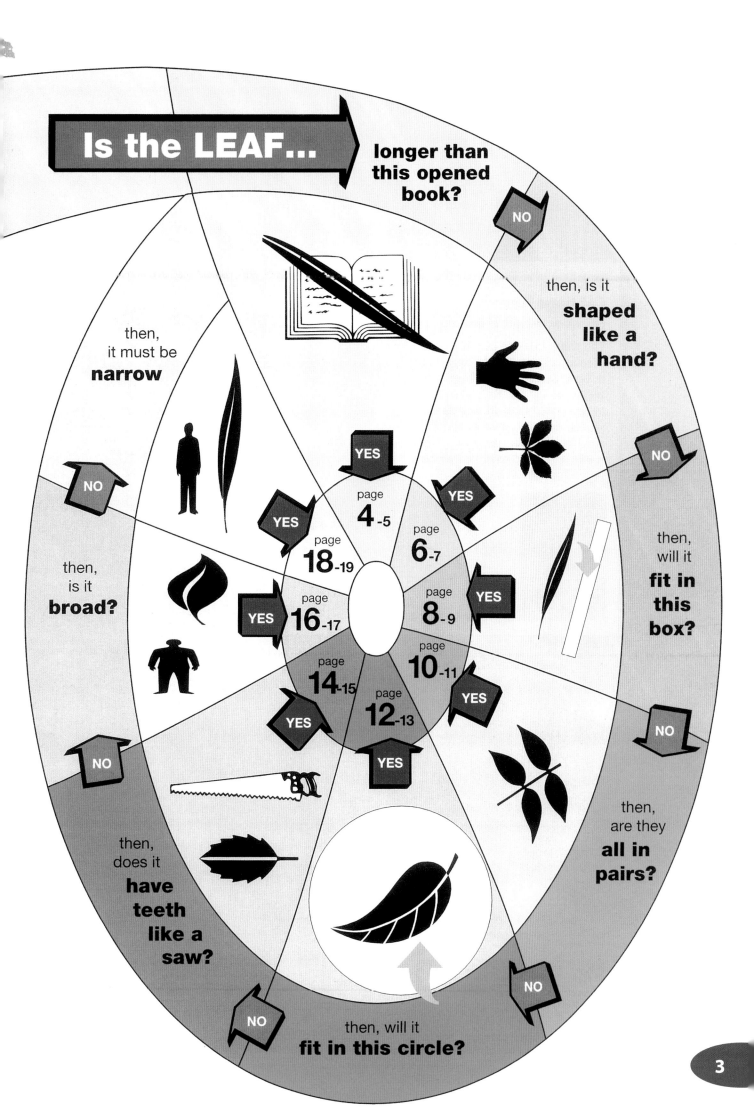

Is the LEAF...

longer than this opened book?

then, it must be **narrow**

then, is it **shaped like a hand?**

then, is it **broad?**

then, will it **fit in this box?**

page **4**-5
page **6**-7
page **8**-9
page **10**-11
page **12**-13
page **14**-15
page **16**-17
page **18**-19

YES / NO labels

then, does it **have teeth like a saw?**

then, are they **all in pairs?**

then, will it **fit in this circle?**

3

Leaves

Ti Kouka
Cabbage Tree
(bark feels like cork to squeeze)

The name 'cabbage tree' has been used for all sorts of palm trees, but in New Zealand the cabbage tree isn't a palm at all. Early Maori ate these cooked tops, as well as the shoots, the cooked roots and the soft inside part of the trunk. The leaves have been used for making paper, rope and string.

cabbage tree trunk

Nikau

(palm leaves; trunk with rings)

Nikau fronds were used to make the roofs of some of the first houses in New Zealand. The rounded bottom end of the frond could also be cut off and used as a bowl. Kereru (New Zealand pigeon) eat the small red fruit, spreading the seeds.

Roof made from woven palm leaf

Pate

(leaves with 7-9 fingers; tiny teeth)

Sometimes called 'seven finger' because the leaves spread out like the fingers of a hand. But you will often find 'seven fingers' with eight or nine fingers! Maori used the soft wood for lighting fires (see kaikomako to learn how). Silvereye, bellbird and tui eat the small dark purple fruit in autumn.

All leaves are life-size. This book works best if you start at page 2.

◀ Puriri moth
(life-size)

Puriri

(leaves with 3-5 fingers; no teeth)

Kereru can swallow the large, round, red puriri berries in one gulp. Tui and kereru drink nectar from the pink flowers. (Look out for old flowers on the ground.) The trunk of the tree often has finger-sized holes in it, which are made by the caterpillars of the large green **puriri moth**.

Whauwhaupaku
Five Finger

(leaves with 5-7 fingers; large teeth)

The leaflets spread like the fingers of a hand. But five finger does not always have five fingers. You will often find them with six or seven. **Possums** chew off the bottom end of the stalk leaving the rest of the leaf to fall. This can eventually kill the tree.

▼ Possum

7

Leaves

Rimu
(leaves spiky to touch)

With its weeping branches, it is a surprise to find rimu leaves feel so stiff and spiky to grab hold of. The wood has often been used for building and making furniture.

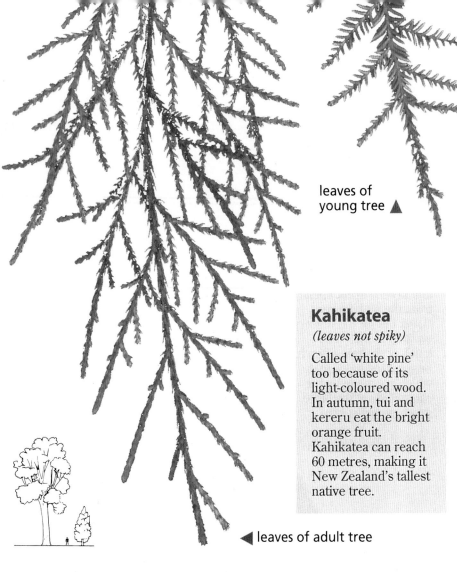

leaves of
young tree ▲

Kahikatea
(leaves not spiky)

Called 'white pine' too because of its light-coloured wood. In autumn, tui and kereru eat the bright orange fruit. Kahikatea can reach 60 metres, making it New Zealand's tallest native tree.

◀ leaves of adult tree

Rimu and Kahikatea
Old trees look a different shape from young ones.

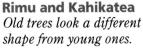

Matai
(leaves lie flat like a feather; whitish underneath)

In summer, kereru eat the large black fruit. The wood was often used for floorboards and is still sometimes used by woodturners.

▼ leaves of young tree

leaves of ▲
adult tree

Miro and Matai ▶
These grow into tall trees.

▲ underside
of leaves

Miro
(leaves lie flat like a feather)

Kereru love to eat the strong-tasting pinkish-purple miro fruit. The wood was once used for building and is sometimes still used for woodcarving.

8

All leaves are life-size. This book works best if you start at page 2.

Totara

(leaves very stiff; spiky to touch)

Waka taua (war canoes) were often carved from one totara tree and the wood is still used for carving today. Also, instead of using matches, a pointed totara stick could be scraped up and down a slab of softer wood (like mahoe) to start a fire. In autumn, tui eat the fruit.

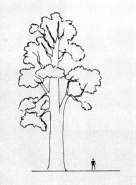

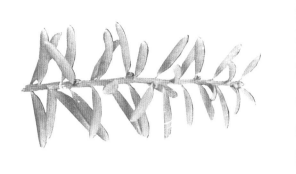

Manuka

(leaves spiky to touch)

Also called 'tea tree' because Captain Cook made tea from the leaves. Manuka twigs were useful for making brooms, while poles were made into paddles and spear handles. Manuka is an important nursery tree, meaning that it often helps to protect other young trees from too much sun and wind.

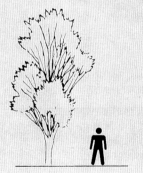

Kanuka

(leaves soft to touch)

Kanuka can grow twice as tall as manuka. Another helpful difference to look for is the flowers and seed capsules. The *larger* kanuka has the *smaller* flowers and seed capsules. Kanuka leaves are usually softer to touch too.

Mingimingi

There are two common kinds of mingimingi. One with narrow prickly leaves, the other with wider softer leaves. Both kinds usually grow as shrubs rather than trees and both have small edible berries.

Wide-Leaved Mingimingi ▼
(leaves wide)

▼ leaves of young plants

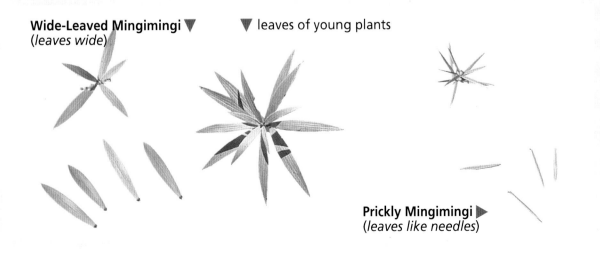

Prickly Mingimingi ▶
(leaves like needles)

Leaves

◀ Kauri
see page 13

◀ Tawa
see page 19

◀ Kowhai
see page 12

Kohekohe
(leaves in 3 or 4 pairs)

Kohekohe flowers are unusual: they sprout straight from the trunk! In many areas, kohekohe trees are disappearing because possums eat their leaves.

Porokaiwhiri Pigeonwood ▶
(leaves with widely spaced teeth)

Pigeons (kereru) flock to the tree in early summer to eat the orange fruit. In November the male flowers have a lovely sweet smell.

Pohutukawa
(leaves velvety white underneath)

Pohutukawa's fluffy red flowers come out around Christmas time, attracting bees, bellbirds and tui. It grows wild only in the northern part of New Zealand.

▲ **underside of leaf**

▲ **Pohutukawa flower**

Rata
(leaves green underneath)

Is rata a vine or a tree? Well, it depends on the rata. Northern rata often starts as a vine but turns into a tree. Southern rata is always a tree. Most of the others are always vines. Rata trees have fluffy red flowers like pohutukawa.

▲ **Northern Rata**

Southern Rata ▶

10

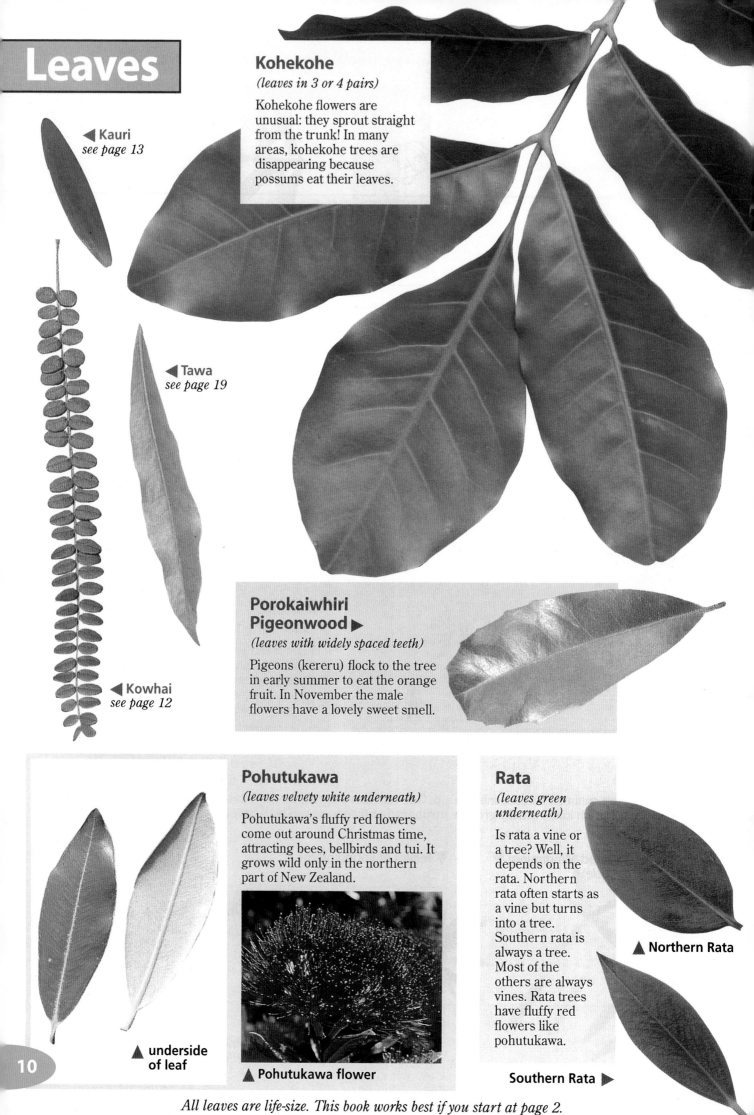

All leaves are life-size. This book works best if you start at page 2.

Pukatea
(square leaf stalks)

Often grows in damp places. Roots are plank-like where they join the trunk. The wood was used for Maori carving.

Kamahi
(leaves have large teeth)

Finger-shaped bunches of tiny white flowers in late spring and early summer. The dried bark was used for tanning leather.

Makomako Wineberry   ▲ underside of leaf

(stalk red and underside of leaf often red)

Wine was made from the dark red or black berries. Tui, silvereye and kereru eat the berries and kereru eat the leaves.

Kawakawa
(leaves heart-shaped, often with holes)

Holes are made in the leaves by looper caterpillars (sometimes seen hiding on the underside of the leaves). The yellow fruit is eaten by kereru.

Shrubs

Shrubs: like a tree but not a tree. Shrubs are usually smaller than trees and don't have a large trunk like trees do.

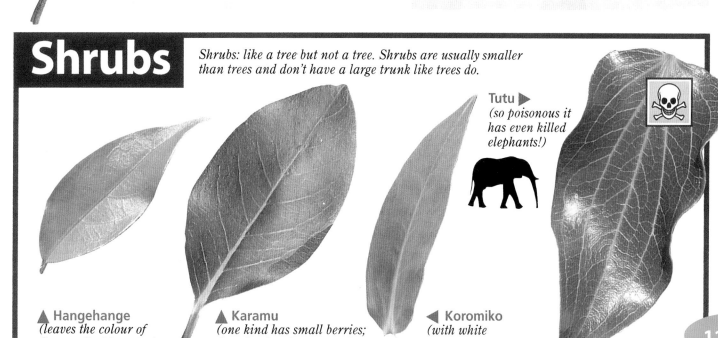

Tutu ▶
(so poisonous it has even killed elephants!)

▲ **Hangehange**
(leaves the colour of Granny Smith apples)

▲ **Karamu**
(one kind has small berries; the other has larger ones)

◀ **Koromiko**
(with white bottlebrush flowers)

Leaves

Tawhai ▶
Silver Beech

Tawhai Rauriki ▶
Mountain Beech

◀ Tawhai Rauriki
Black Beech

Tawhai Raunui ▲
Hard Beech

Tawhai Raunui ▲
Red Beech

Beech

There are five kinds of native beech trees. Some are so similar that even the experts have trouble telling them apart! Many were important timber trees.

Tanekaha

(leaves like celery leaves)

Also called 'celery pine' because its leaves look rather like celery leaves. The stems of young tanekaha used to be sent to London for making walking sticks.

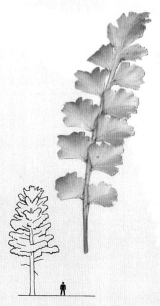

Kowhai

(small leaves in two long rows)

In early spring kowhai's large drooping yellow flowers attract tui and bellbird. Kereru eat the leaves and flowers. Its little hard yellow seeds can float huge distances across the sea and still be able to grow.

There are two different kinds of kowhai. They have different leaves. (below left and right)

Putaputaweta

(smaller leaves on young trees)

▼ leaf of adult tree

Also called marbleleaf. 'Putaputaweta' means 'full of weta holes', because the tree trunk often has holes in it that **weta** live in. But the holes are really made by other insects, like the caterpillars of the puriri moth (see page 7).

leaves of young tree ▲

weta live in the hole (life-size) ▶

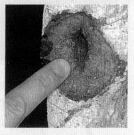

puriri moth hole ▲

leaves of young tree ▶

leaf of ▲ adult tree

Kaikomako

(smaller leaves on young trees)

Kaikomako means 'food of the bellbird'; they eat the small black berries. Maori used the wood for lighting fires. They scraped a pointed stick of kaikomako up and down a slab of dry softer wood (like pate or mahoe) until the fine wood dust started to smoulder.

All leaves are life-size. This book works best if you start at page 2.

Kauri
(leaves mostly 2-4 cm, longer on young trees)

Kauri is one of the largest trees in the world. The largest one ever found was 26.8 metres around the trunk – about twice as wide as the one in the picture – and more than 2,000 years old. Kauri wood was used for building and the **gum** that bleeds from the tree was collected for making varnish.

▲ young kauri tree

▲ kauri gum

◀ Mingimingi
(when young)
see page 9

▲ The Yakas Kauri

This is the seventh largest kauri alive today, 13.2 metres around and about 1200 years old. A rough guide to the age of a kauri is to imagine how many ten-year old children it would take to hug it and then multiply by 100 years.

Kohuhu
(young stems black)

Early Maori used the leaves as a perfume, putting them in a little bag to hang around the neck. (Crush a leaf and smell.) Gardeners often call this tree *Pittosporum*, which means 'sticky seeds'. There are other kinds of *Pittosporum* (see tarata, page 18).

Mapou
(young stems red)

Looks similar to kohuhu, except that mapou has red stems. Silvereye, tui and whitehead eat the small black berries. Look out for young mapou growing beneath the trees where these birds have perched.

Leaves

Titoki
see page 18

Kaikomako ▶
see page 12

Hinau

(leaves whitish underneath, edges curled so teeth can be hard to see)

White bell-shaped flowers in spring. In autumn, the dark purple berries attract kereru. Maori made pudding-like cakes from the flesh of these berries and used the bark to make a black dye for colouring flax.

▲ underside of leaf

Ngaio

(hold a leaf to the light to see the pale dots)

The tiny clear dots in the leaves contain a poison which Maori used for stopping sandflies and mosquitoes from biting. They did this by rubbing their bodies with the sticky black shoots or washing themselves in a tea made from the leaves.

leaf held up to the light *(not life-size)*

Houhere Lacebark

(leaves have large sharp teeth)

The European name comes from the fine, lacy layer of fibres that grow under the bark. This 'lace' was used by Maori for making rope, cloth, hats and headbands. Houhere has large white flowers in late summer and autumn. Kereru eat the leaves.

the 'lace' that gives lacebark its name ▶

Kotukutuku
see page 19

14

All leaves are life-size. This book works best if you start at page 2.

Horoeka
Lancewood
(leaves thick like leather)

Young trees have no branches and are as straight as a lance. But the tree and its leaves change completely as it grows. The central strips of young leaves were used as bootlaces.

adult tree

▼ young tree

▲ leaf of adult tree

◄ leaf of young tree

Rewarewa
(new shoots covered in brown fuzz)

Also called 'New Zealand honeysuckle' because the nectar is easily sucked from the flowers. Bees, bellbird, silvereye and tui drink this too. In late spring, the curled up red-and-yellow flowers fall to the ground.

◄ leaf of adult tree

leaf of young tree ►

leaf skeleton *(seen on the ground)*

Mahoe
Whiteywood
(trunk often has white patches)

Look out for leaf skeletons – dead leaves that have partly rotted to leave a pretty, lacy pattern of veins. (These look great photocopied.) In late summer, tui, silvereye and whitehead eat the small purple berries.

◄ The white patches on the trunk give whiteywood its name.

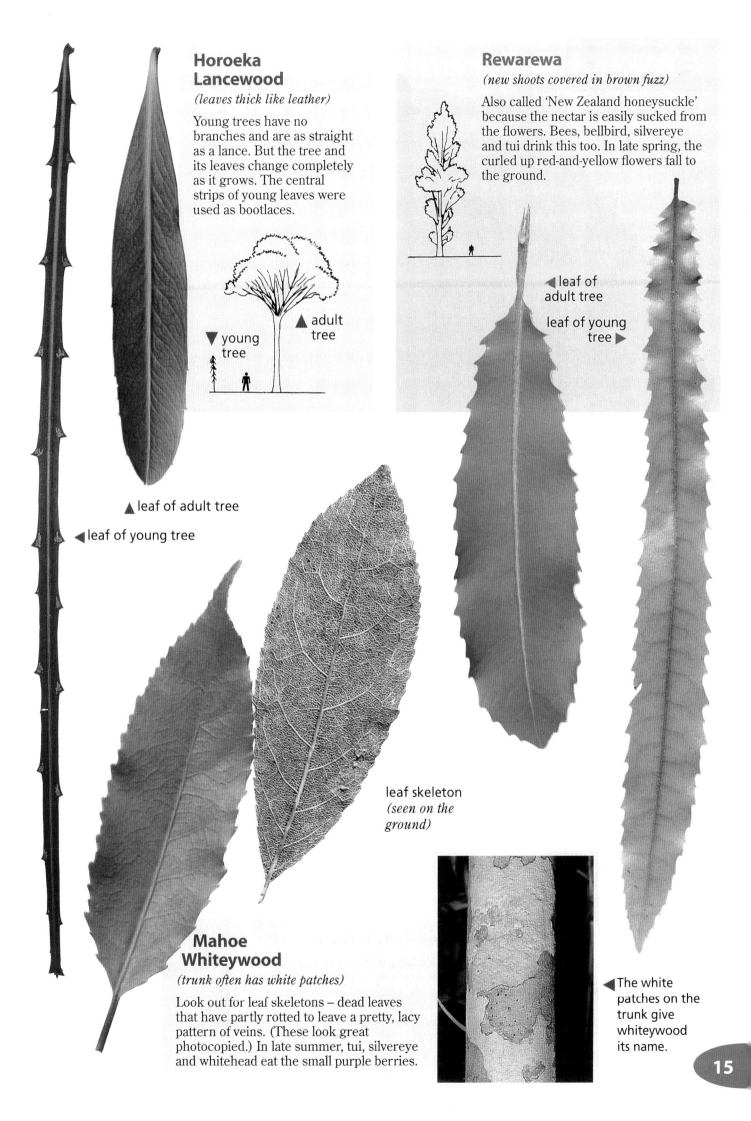

underside of leaf ▲

Rangiora

(leaves very large, white underneath)

Sometimes called bushman's toilet paper because its leaves can be useful in an emergency! They also make good leaf boats and great notepaper (felts and biro work best). Maori used them too, either as bandages on wounds and sores, or for wrapping up hangi meals. Rangiora gum is poisonous.

Rangiora used as notepaper

All leaves are life-size. This book works best if you start at page 2.

Karaka
(leaves glossy; edges tightly curled)

Although kereru safely eat the large orange fruit, the raw seed is very poisonous to humans. Early Maori cooked these seeds for a long time and soaked them to destroy the poison and make them safe to eat.

Karaka fruit
(poisonous)

Taraire
(brown fuzz on new shoots; leaves pale underneath)

Only grows naturally in the north of New Zealand. Has large purple-black fruit that kereru like to eat. The large cooked seeds were also eaten by early Maori: when roasted, they taste like potato.

▲ underside of leaf

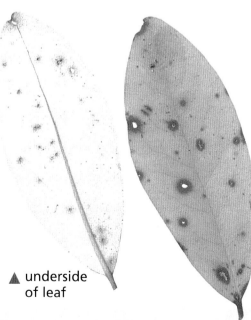

▲ underside of leaf

Horopito
(leaves smell strongly when crushed; pale beneath)

This can be a shrub or a small tree. Also sometimes called 'pepper tree' because of the hot spicy taste of the leaves. These leaves can be chewed to relieve toothache.

Puka
Shining Broadleaf ▼
(leaves very lop-sided and glossy)

▲ **Kapuka**
Common Broadleaf
(leaves dull underneath)

Broadleaf

Common broadleaf grows on the ground. But shining broadleaf is much trickier to find because it usually perches high up in other trees. Shining broadleaf has very glossy leaves much longer on one side than on the other.

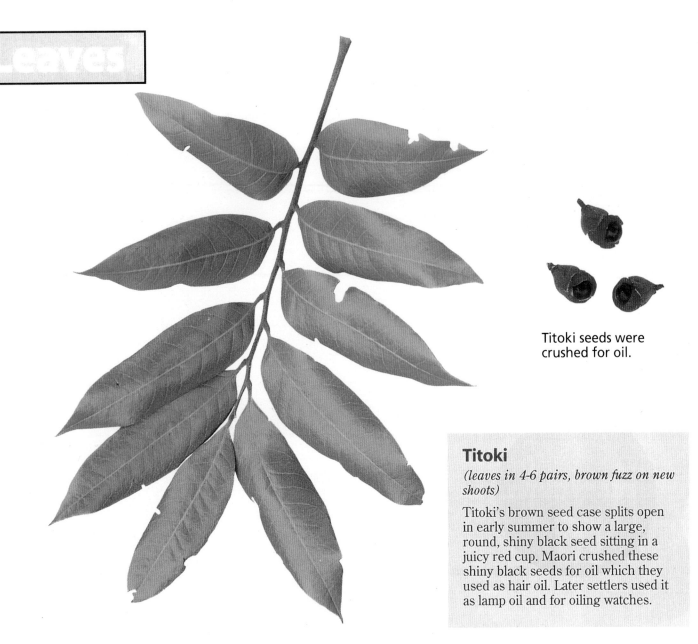

Titoki seeds were
crushed for oil.

Titoki

*(leaves in 4-6 pairs, brown fuzz on new
shoots)*

Titoki's brown seed case splits open
in early summer to show a large,
round, shiny black seed sitting in a
juicy red cup. Maori crushed these
shiny black seeds for oil which they
used as hair oil. Later settlers used it
as lamp oil and for oiling watches.

Tarata
Lemonwood

(crushed leaves smell of lemon)

Crush a leaf between your fingers to discover a smell like lemons or
carrots. Maori collected these crushed leaves and the sweet-smelling
cream-coloured flowers (in late spring) for making scented body oil.

All leaves are life-size. This book works best if you start at page 2.

Kotukutuku Tree Fuchsia

(leaves white underneath)

The largest fuchsia in the world. Maori ate the small black berries and later settlers used them to make puddings and jam. Some people even squeezed them for making ink. Kereru, tui and whitehead eat these too. In spring, bellbird, silvereye and tui drink the nectar from the pretty purple flowers. Look for the tree's loose papery bark.

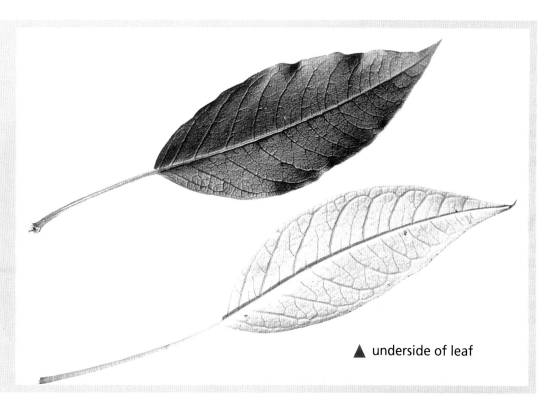

▲ underside of leaf

Akeake

(leaves sandpapery to touch)

Akeake wood was used by early Maori for making weapons and tools. It is so hard that if you try to cut it with an axe, the axe will often just bounce off the wood. There is also a garden akeake with purple leaves.

Hinau
see page 14

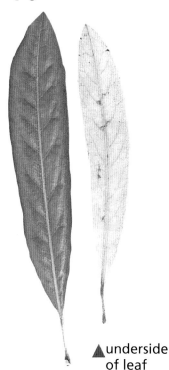

▲underside of leaf

Tawa

(new shoots covered in brown fuzz)

Kereru and kaka eat the large purple fruit in late summer. The cooked seeds of this fruit were eaten by Maori too, and taste like potato. The wood was used by Maori for making bird spears and by Europeans for making clothes pegs, barrels and buckets.

underside of leaf ▼

19

Flowers which colour?

Flowers attract birds, lizards, bats and insects to drink their sweet nectar. When these creatures take the nectar they pick up pollen dust too, and carry this to the next flower they visit. This makes new seeds which grow into new plants, and is called pollination.

White flowers

are mostly pollinated by beetles, moths, flies and small native bees, for they can see this colour easily, especially at night. Geckos pollinate some white flowers and some coloured ones too.

Lacebark
see page 14

Clematis
see page 26

Common green gecko

This lizard eats the nectar of manuka flowers and is one of the creatures that pollinates them.

Manuka
see page 9

Kanuka
see page 9

Bush Lawyer
see page 26

Koromiko
see page 11

Ngaio ▶
see page 14

Hinau
see page 14

Kohekohe
see page 10

▲ Putaputaweta
see page 12

Kamahi
see page 11

◀ Small White Rata Vine
see page 26

All flowers are life-size.

Large, brightly coloured flowers

Are usually pollinated by birds, for they find these colours attractive. The **tui**, for example, takes nectar from many of these bright flowers.

Kowhai ▶
see page 12

▲ **Tarata**
see page 18

◀ **Wineberry**
see page 11

Taurepo ▼
(a forest shrub)

Karapapa ▼
(a forest shrub)

Puriri ▲
see page 7

Pohutukawa or Rata Tree *see page 10*

Rata Vine ▶
see page 26

Nikau ▶
see page 5

▲ **Kotukutuku**
see page 19

Rewarewa ▶
see page 15

Kohuhu ▲
see page 13

21

Berries which colour?

Fruit eaters and seed travel

Berries are eaten by birds and lizards. These help the tree by carrying its seeds somewhere else where they can grow into new trees.

The **kereru** (New Zealand pigeon) is particularly important for spreading seeds because it can eat the largest forest fruits without breaking up the seed.

▼ **Kawakawa**
see page 11

▲ **Karaka**
(raw seed **poisonous**)
see page 17

Tutu ▶
(poisonous)
see page 11

◀ **Five Finger**
see page 7

▲ **Bush Lawyer**
see page 26

▲ **Pigeonwood**
see page 10

Tawa ▶
see page 19

◀ **Mahoe**
see page 15

◀ **Karamu**
see page 11

▲ **Titoki**
see page 18

▼ **Turutu**
see page 28

◀ **Nikau**
see page 5

▲ **Hinau**
see page 14

▲ **Taraire**
see page 17

Totara ▼
see page 9

Kahikatea ▲
see page 8

Kotukutuku ▶
see page 19

◀ **Mingimingi**
(broad-leaved)
see page 9

▲ **Supplejack**
see page 26

▼ **Puriri**
see page 7

▼ **Miro**
see page 8

◀ **Mingimingi** ▶
(prickly)
see page 9

22

All seeds and berries are life-size.

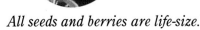

Other Seeds which kind?

How do other seeds travel?

Fluffy or flaky seeds are carried by the wind. Some seeds are sticky or have hooks so they can hitch-hike on the fur or feathers of animals. Some float or have pods that burst to throw their seeds out.

flaky seeds in a cone

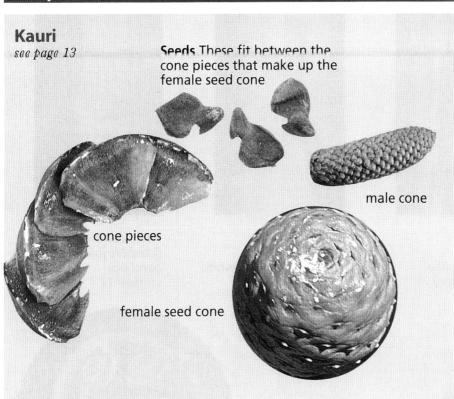

Kauri
see page 13

Seeds These fit between the cone pieces that make up the female seed cone

male cone

cone pieces

female seed cone

hard seeds in a pod

Kowhai
see page 12

To get these seeds to sprout, you will need to leave them in hot water for 90 minutes or use a knife to cut off an edge of the seed coat.

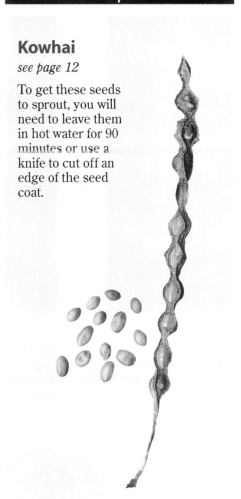

sticky seeds in a capsule

Tarata and Kohuhu
see pages 18 and 13

flaky seeds in a pod

Rewarewa
see page 15

fluffy seeds in a capsule

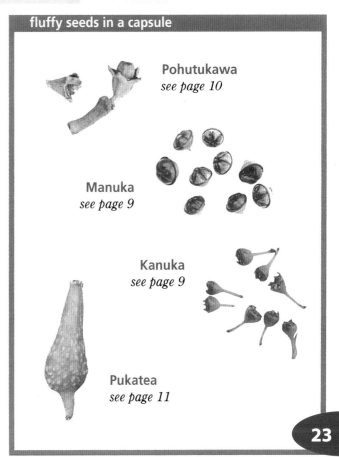

Pohutukawa
see page 10

Manuka
see page 9

Kanuka
see page 9

Pukatea
see page 11

other flaky seeds

Lacebark
see page 14

Akeake
see page 19

23

Trunk & Bark

(some special trunks to look out for)

Nikau
(green, brown or grey trunk with rings)
These rings are left by the falling fronds.
see page 5

Horoeka

(trunk looks like stretched rope)
see page 15

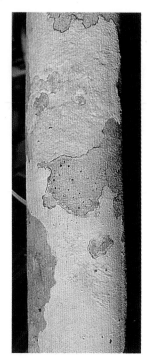

Mahoe

(trunk with many white patches)
see page 15

Kawakawa
(knobbly joints like bamboo)
see page 11

Cicada

Rows of arrowhead cuts are made in the branches of many trees by the **cicada** as it pushes its eggs deep inside.

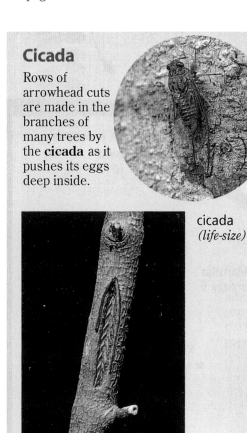

cicada
(life-size)

Tree ferns

There are many kinds of tree ferns. All have coiled shoots. Two common ones are:

Mamaku
(thick black frond stalks)
New Zealand's largest tree fern, reaching 20 metres.

Ponga
(white frond stalks)
National emblem, the silver fern – the fronds are silvery white underneath.

Forest Giants

(The leaves of these trees are usually hard to reach. If you can reach a leaf, go back to page 3.)

Kauri page 13
(hammer-marked)
like the bark of a
Matai – below – or
Miro page 8

Rimu page 8
(flaky)
like the bark of a
Kahikatea page 8
or **Rata** page 10

Matai page 8
(hammer-marked)

Totara page 9
(stringy)

Native timber

Many people don't realise that New Zealand's native forests are still being cut down. If you spot native timbers being used, don't be afraid to ask questions.

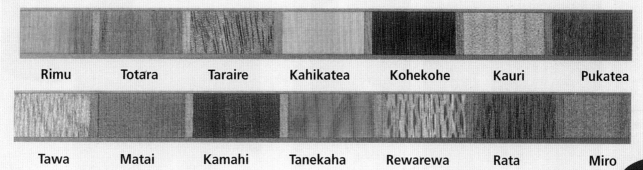

| Rimu | Totara | Taraire | Kahikatea | Kohekohe | Kauri | Pukatea |

| Tawa | Matai | Kamahi | Tanekaha | Rewarewa | Rata | Miro |

Climbers

Kareao
Supplejack
(black woody stems)

Climbs by coiling its stems around its support.

Puawananga
Clematis

Climbs by coiling its leaf stalks around its support.

Rata Vine
(flowers like a rata tree)

This rata spends its whole life as a vine. There are other kinds too – with white flowers. Uses clinging roots to climb.

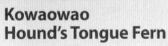

Kowaowao
Hound's Tongue Fern
(young frond looks like a dog's tongue)

Has clinging roots.

Tataramoa
Bush Lawyer
(thorns and fruit like blackberry)

A climber that uses hooks.

Bush Lawyer
thorns ▲
(magnified)

Kiekie
(fruit usually in groups of three)

The flowers show up at night and are probably pollinated by **bats.** Climbs with clinging roots.

▲ fruit

flower ▶

◀ short-tailed bat

Perching plants

Where to look

Some perching plants cling to the *trunks* of trees. Others are found growing on the *branches* overhead.

Old Man's Beard Lichen
Lichens like this don't usually harm the tree.

Peka-a-Waka Bamboo Orchid

(sweet-smelling flowers in spring)

Golden Foliose Lichen
(golden underneath)
'Foliose' means it looks like a leaf.

Leafy Liverwort
(looks like a moss)

Unlike mosses, leafy liverwort leaves are arranged in two neat rows and have no vein.

Kahakaha Perching Lily

Collects water like a funnel, growing some of its roots backwards to get a drink.

Orange Bracket Fungus
(hard, like wood)

Makawe Hanging Spleenwort Fern

Makawe means 'hanging like hair'.

Moss
(soft, green and fluffy)

Most moss leaves have a tiny vein running along the middle (unlike leafy liverworts).

Filmy Fern
(see-through fronds)

Bracket Fungus
(hard, like wood)

Also sometimes called shelf fungus.

Hakeka Ear Fungus
(rubbery to touch)

Popular in China as food and for medicine.

Forest floor

plants that grow beneath the trees

Kamu
Hook Grass

The hooked seeds often get caught in your socks. Before socks and people came to New Zealand, the seeds could still hitch-hike on the feathers of kiwi.

▲ hook grass seed
(magnified)

Mapere
Cutty Grass

Leaves cut your skin if you rub against them. (Look at a leaf under a microscope, to see the thousands of tiny sharp teeth.) **Kiwi** often sleep beneath the plants.

Turutu
Blueberry

The pale blue to purple berries (found in summer) contain an inky juice.

Ferns

The new shoot of most ferns is coiled like the koru in Maori carving. ▶

◀ Piupiu
Crown Fern

(fronds whitish underneath)

This is one of the common forest ferns, but there are many others.

Tutukiwi
Hooded Orchid

Touch inside of flower (found in spring) and watch what happens. Click! This trigger flicks insects inside to pollinate the flower. The trigger takes 15 minutes to reset.

Nertera
With tiny red berries in summer and autumn.

Panakenake Pratia
Has unusual 'half-flowers' late spring to early autumn.

Parataniwha
(leaves often reddish-purple)
A nettle that doesn't sting.

Scarlet Pixie-Cup Lichen
Often found on rotting wood, sometimes on the ground. Its common name comes from the bright red tips which can look like tiny cups.

Raurenga Kidney Fern
(see-through fronds, shaped like kidneys)

➡ For young trees, go back to page 3

➡ For fungi of the forest floor, turn to page 30

Fungi are different from ordinary plants because they don't have green leaves or need sunlight to grow. They come in many shapes and in all the colours of the rainbow. Although some are poisonous, it is quite safe to touch them.

Green Wax-Gill
(as green as a leaf)

Blue-Cap
(as blue as the sky)
The blue *Entoloma*.

Purple Pouch Fungus
Common in native beech forest.

Yellow Wax-Gill
(as yellow as a lemon)

Orange Pore Fungus
(like a fan with pores on one side)

A tropical fungus that has recently become very common here.

Red Wax-Gill
(as red as a tomato)

Called a wax-gill because the gills beneath the cap feel waxy to touch.

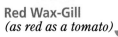

**▲ Tututupo
Toothpaste Fungus**

A kind of fairy club fungus that seems to ooze out of the ground like pinky orange toothpaste.

▼ Coral Fungus
(thick branched clumps)

A kind of fungus that looks like coral.

**▲ Paruwhatitiri
Basket Fungus**
(the 'basket' can be 15 cm across)

Rolled along the ground by the wind, spreading its spores.

◀ Bird's Nest Fungus
(found on dead twigs)

A drop of rain hitting the 'nest' throws out the flat white 'eggs' to spread their spores.

**▲ Puapua-a-Autahi
Flower Fungus**

Bursts from its shell, stretching out smelly red arms like a flower. The smell attracts flies which spread the sticky spores.

**▼ Awhato
Vegetable Caterpillar**
(only the brown spore stalk shows above ground)

A fungus which feeds on an underground caterpillar, turning its body hard, like wood.

▲ Velvet Earthstar
The thick outside shell peels back to leave a neat star with another puffball inside.

All fungi are life-size.

Slime Mould

Because a hungry slime mould can creep along at 2 or 3 cm per hour, (5 cm per hour if it is in a hurry), they are sometimes called 'fungus animals'. But slime moulds are not really animals. Most live on the forest floor, feeding on bacteria and fungi.

Slime moulds can travel this far in one hour

▣ Glossary

alga   (**Algae** if there is more than one.) A large group of plants with no flowers. Most of them live in water.

fern   A large group of plants without flowers. Most have large divided leaves, called fronds, and tightly coiled new shoots.

frond   The leaf of a fern or a palm.

fungus   (**Fungi** if there is more than one.) Although most people think of fungi as plants, scientists say that they are too different from other plants to call them true plants. They are protista.

lichen   Pronounced *like-en*. A large group of flowerless plants, most of which are a partnership of an alga living on a fungus.

liverwort A large group of flowerless plants. The leafy ones look like mosses but the others look fleshy like a piece of squashed liver.

moss   A large group of flowerless plants. Most moss leaves have a tiny vein running along the middle. (Liverworts don't.)

native plant A plant found in this country, but not brought here by people.

nectar   The sweet, watery, honey-like liquid found inside a flower.

pollen   A fine powder inside a flower that is used for pollination.

shrub   A woody plant with no trunk, usually smaller than a tree.

spore   The dust-like seed of a fern, fungus, moss etc.

tree   A large woody plant with a trunk (usually bigger than a shrub).

▣ Useful Books

Mushrooms & Toadstools (Mobil NZ Nature) by Marie Taylor, Reed, 1981.

Native Forests and Trees by Gordon Ell, Bush Press, 1985.

The Introduced Common Trees of New Zealand by Gordon Ell, Bush Press, 1984.

Tree (Collins Eyewitness Guides) by David Burnie, HarperCollins, Australia, 1988.

What's Going on in the Bush? by Donna Bryant, Hodder & Stoughton, 1993.

Which Native Fern? by Andrew Crowe, Penguin, 1994.

Which Native Forest Plant? by Andrew Crowe, Penguin, 1994.

Which Native Tree? by Andrew Crowe, Penguin, 1992.

Index

Where there are several page numbers, the bold number shows the main entry.